My Name is Clara

A Collection of Stories about People who Share my Name

By Allison Dearstyne

For Clara Noel, my girl who brightens every room she enters.

The name Clara is Latin. It came from Ancient Rome, in present-day Italy. "Clara" came from the boy's name "Clarus," which means clear or bright. The girl's name Clara was made famous about 800 years ago by Saint Clara of Assisi, who joyfully gave up her wealth to become a nun and serve others.

In Johanna Spyri's novel *Heidi*, Clara Sesemann is Heidi's wheelchair-bound friend. In Tchaikovsky's ballet *The Nutcracker*, Clara is the little girl who dreams of a living nutcracker and travels with him to the land of sugar plum fairies. You can always hear music from *The Nutcracker* around Christmastime.

There have been heroes named Clara around the world through history! We will look at these seven remarkable women who share your name: Clara Barton, Clara Brown, Clara Bow, Clara Hughes, Clara Schumann, Clara Immerwahr and and Clara Breed.

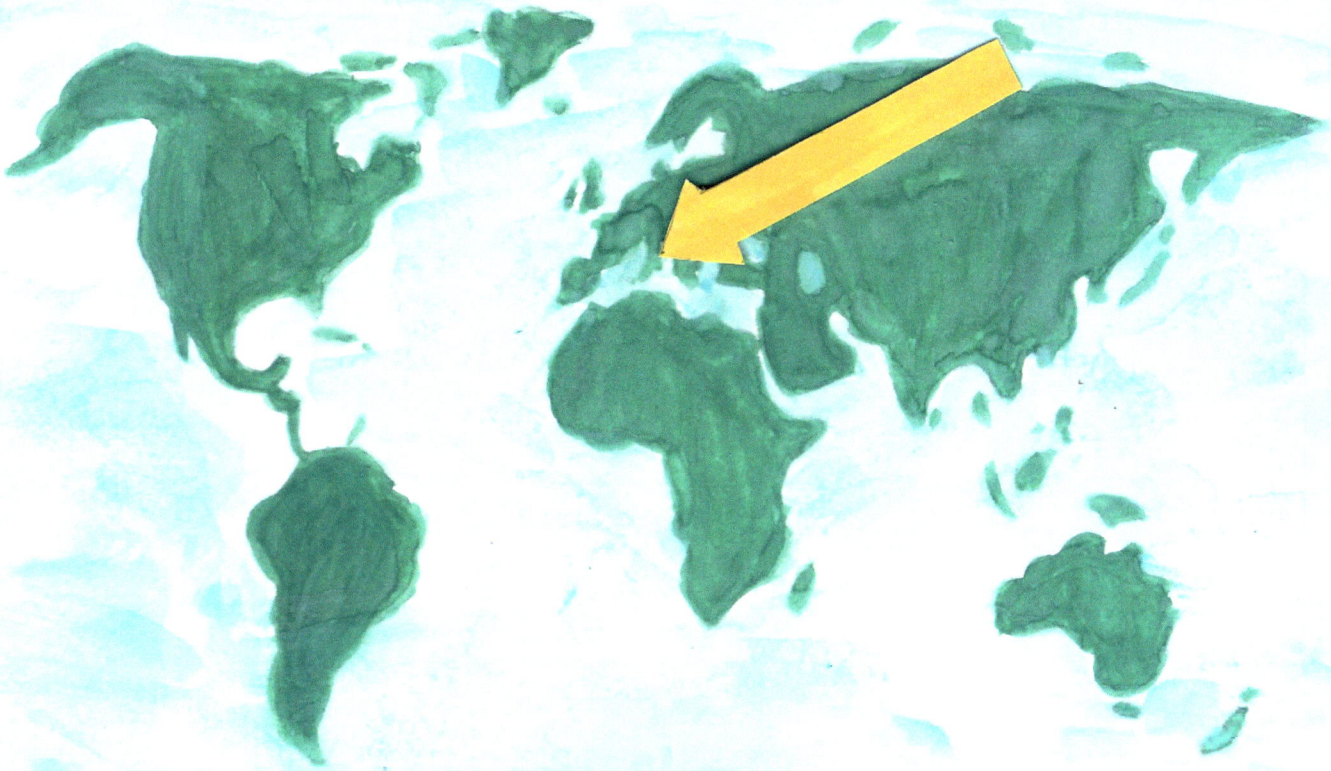

Clarissa "Clara" Barton was a shy little girl who grew up to do big things! She was born on Christmas Day in Massachusetts in 1821, the youngest of five children. When Clara Barton went to school, she did not make any friends for years because she was so painfully shy. Her parents spent her whole childhood trying unsuccessfully to help her overcome her shyness.

When Clara Barton was ten years old, her brother fell off the roof of a barn! The doctors said there was nothing they could do to save him and gave up. But Clara Barton did not give up! She surprised everyone by nursing her brother back to health. Her early practice helping her brother gave her some medical skills that she would use again as an adult!

She took on another project to help a widowed relative repair her home and found that she was happy when she helped others in need. She played mostly with her boy cousins and rode horses like them, which was not considered fitting for a young lady back in those days. Clara Barton's mother told her she had to play with her girl cousins instead to become a proper lady.

When she was 17 years old, her parents encouraged her to become a teacher to help her overcome her shyness. She was an excellent teacher and did especially well handling squirrelly little boys. As a former tomboy, she related to them and gained their respect. She was so successful that the headmaster wanted her to teach more days throughout the year but pay her less than men teachers. When Clara Barton boldly demanded that she get paid the same as the men, they agreed to pay her the full wage.

Later she earned a degree in teaching and worked in a private school. In the meantime, she took on big projects like campaigning to allow children of workers to go to school. Back in those days, children were not protected by child labor laws, and many had to go to work like their parents.

When she noticed a city in New Jersey with no public schools, she offered to teach local children for free! She explained that although she deserved a man's wages for the job she did, she would be willing to teach those in need for nothing. Eventually 600 children came to learn! The city officials finally saw the importance of education and raised enough money for a school building. She was the headmaster of the school she founded until the school board voted to replace her with a man, simply because she was a woman. It wasn't fair!

So, Clara Barton gave up teaching and moved to Washington, D.C. to work for the United States government as a clerk. She became the first woman to earn the same amount of money as men in the same position. The male clerks were not kind to her. She was fired under President James Buchanan, and then re-hired under President Abraham Lincoln who sided with her, wanting equality in the workplace. She paved the way for more women to work for the government.

In 1861, her plans changed when the American Civil War began. Eager to serve her country, she jumped into action, helping wounded soldiers and putting ads in local papers to get supplies for the Union Army. Brave Clara Barton often risked her life running onto battlefields to care for wounded soldiers. As she tended them, she recognized some of the soldiers as her former students.

There wasn't any special training program for nurses back in those days, so Clara Barton taught herself how to be a nurse! She was called the "Angel of the Battlefield" because of the comfort she gave to so many soldiers. After the war was over, she helped families of fallen soldiers by identifying and properly burying the soldiers in marked graves.

Then she traveled around the country giving speeches about her experiences in war. She taught first-aid skills to anyone willing to learn. She became friends with Susan B. Anthony, who inspired her to fight for women's right to vote. Her friend Frederick Douglass inspired her to fight for equal rights for Black Americans. Clara Barton was unstoppable!

Later, Clara Barton founded the American Red Cross to help people who needed medical care during wartime and natural disasters. To this day, the American Red Cross does just that and more! In her lifetime, three different men wanted to marry her, but Clara Barton remained happily single.

Because she was one of the first ladies to do so many things, we call her a pioneer. Maybe you will be a pioneer like Clara Barton!

Clara Brown was a slave who learned to make lemonade out of lemons. That means she took a hardship in her life and made something wonderful out of it. Clara Brown was born in 1800 in Virginia. She grew up farming tobacco alongside her mother and other slaves.

During her childhood, she and her mother moved with their masters to Kentucky. There, she married another slave, Richard, and together they had four children. Clara Brown and Richard raised their children together for 17 years, and then their master died. She and her family were sold at an auction, where they were all tragically separated from each other. Clara Brown would never stop looking for her family.

Years later when Clara Brown's second master died, she was granted her freedom. She was 56 years old then, and slavery was still legal in the United States. There was a law that she couldn't live as a free woman in Kentucky, so Clara Brown walked west to Colorado. There, she worked as a laundress, cook and midwife.

Clara Brown wisely invested the money she made from her jobs to buy land and gold mines in towns nearby. These investments made a lot of money for her! With her new wealth, she was generous. She opened her home to the community, allowing it to be used as a church, hospital and home for the poor. Although she experienced discrimination as a Black woman, Clara Brown joyfully served everyone.

She used to say, "I always go where Jesus calls me." Clara Brown became lovingly known as "Aunt Clara" because she took care of the needs of so many others.

When the Civil War ended, Clara Brown was allowed to freely travel. So, she sold everything she had to go back to Kentucky to search for her family. It took her almost 20 years, but finally when she was 82 years old, Clara Brown found one of her daughters, Eliza Jane. Their reunion filled them both with joy!

In the meantime, she paid the way for 16 other relatives and former slave friends to move to Colorado. She also helped pay for a large group of freed slaves to build a community in Kansas. As an old lady, she was frail and had nearly run out of money from giving so much to so many. But Clara Brown was rich where it counted!

Her last years were happy, as she spent them with her daughter and kept her anchor of faith in God. During the last year of her life, she was voted into the Society of Colorado Pioneers because of her special role in the state's early history.

Clara Brown was remarkable in every way. If you find yourself going through a struggle, be inspired by Clara Brown!

Clara Bow was an unlikely American movie star. In 1905 she was born in New York City to a poor family and was so sick that she was not expected to survive infancy. When she was little, other girls were unkind to her because her clothes were shabby. Most of her friends were boys and she often got into fights.

For a girl to behave this way was considered improper, and people often looked down on her. Despite what others thought, Clara Bow wanted to be a movie star when she was 16. She used to go to the movies and then hurry home to act out the parts of every character in front of her mirror.

She auditioned for some movies, and it didn't go well at first. The producers often told Clara Bow she was too fat to be a movie star. But she knew they were wrong, and she kept pursuing her dream. Finally, Clara Bow was given the chance to act in the silent film *Down to the Sea in Ships*. Critics loved her and said she stole the show even though she wasn't the main character. Her roles in silent films got bigger over the next few years. In total, she acted in 46 silent films. One of the silent films she acted in, *Wings*, won the first ever Academy Award for Best Picture.

In 1929, just five years after Clara Bow became a silent movie star, new technology introduced sound into movies. The new movies were called "talkies" and changed the way movie stars had to act. Clara Bow continued a successful acting career, even with the big change on screen. Her appearance as a spirited shopgirl in the film *It* brought her fame worldwide and earned her the nickname "The 'It' Girl." Producers wanted to hire her because they knew if she was starring in a movie, it would be a blockbuster hit!

Clara Bow was a flapper, which means she dressed and acted in a new fashionable way in the 1920s. She came to be a symbol of the Roaring Twenties. She retired from her acting career at age 28, then married and had children. She and her family settled down on a ranch to live a quiet life. In 1960, Clara Bow was awarded a motion picture star on the Hollywood Walk of Fame.

Clara Bow wasn't afraid to go after her dream, even though so many people underestimated her. The next time you play charades, think about Clara Bow acting in silent movies!

Clara Hughes is a Canadian Olympic medalist who holds a unique record. She was born in 1972 in Winnipeg. As a young teenager, she made bad choices like smoking and doing drugs, and never saw herself becoming the great athlete that she later became.

That all changed for her when she witnessed the great Canadian speed skater Gaétan Boucher at the 1988 Winter Olympics. His races inspired her to kick her bad habits and instead hit the ice to try speed skating. She began riding her bike too and realized that she was a natural athlete.

She competed in the 1996 Summer Olympics and won two bronze medals for women's road cycling. After that, Clara Hughes focused again on speed skating. She competed in the 2002, 2006 and 2010 Winter Olympics and between them won the gold, silver and two bronze medals in speed skating.

What makes Clara Hughes unique is her record in winning medals in both the Summer and Winter Olympics. Only six people in the world have ever won a medal in both the Summer and Winter Olympics. She is the only person in the history of the Olympics to win multiple medals in both!

Her story doesn't end with being a great athlete. She does a lot of work for "The Right to Play." This international organization helps children in need by teaching them to play educational games. Their goal is to make learning fun, and train leaders in communities affected by war, disease, and poverty. She also organized a yearly bike ride across Canada to raise awareness for mental health.

Making a choice to turn her life around and make healthy choices makes Clara Hughes a very strong person, even without her special world record. The next time you hop on a bicycle or put on a pair of skates, think about athletic Clara Hughes!

Clara Schumann was a talented German pianist and composer who lived and breathed music all her life. She was born Clara Weick in 1819 to musical parents. Her mother was a singer and her father played instruments. Her parents divorced when she was five and after that she lived with her father, Friedrich Wieck.

He structured every detail of her daily routine. He gave little Clara lessons for one hour every day in piano, violin, singing, musical theory and composition. Every day after lessons, she practiced for two hours. Clara Schumann's favorite instrument was the piano, and she became so good at the playing it, she became known as a child prodigy. That means she had an extraordinary talent, even as a child!

When she was eight, she played publicly, and in the audience was another young pianist, Robert Schumann. He was so amazed by her playing that he stopped studying law to take lessons from Clara's father. He and Clara became friends, and when Clara turned 21, they married.

Together they became friends with another musician, Johannes Brahms. They told him how gifted he was and built his confidence in composing music. Composing means creating music in your head and writing it out on paper, as sheet music. With encouragement from the Schumanns, Johannes Brahms composed wonderful music. Clara Schumann was the first person to play his songs publicly and helped make his music popular.

One of the most remarkable things about Clara Schumann is that she was one of the first pianists to play piano concerts from memory, without using any sheet music. This was different from most musicians, who read the musical notes as they played. She created her own musical style, and people liked it so much that they requested that other musicians play in her style as well!

Clara Schumann enjoyed a long career playing the piano at concerts for 61 years. She was one of the most famous pianists of her time. We learn from Clara Schumann that hard work pays off! Learn to play a song on the piano by memory and you can be like talented Clara Schumann!

Clara Immerwahr was a chemist who helped pave the way for other women to become scientists. She was born in Poland in 1870, the youngest daughter to Jewish parents. Her father was a successful chemist and she followed in his footsteps. Clara Immerwahr attended college and was the first woman to earn a doctorate in chemistry in Germany. Mostly she studied salts that were found in different types of metal.

After she earned her degree, she married another chemist, Fritz Haber. Back in those days, married women were expected to stay in the home while their husbands worked other jobs. Because of this, she couldn't continue her research like she wanted. Instead, she helped her husband with his work and never earned recognition for it.

During World War I, her husband created weapons used by the Germans and won a Nobel Prize in chemistry for his work. Clara Immerwahr was horrified by the role he played in such a devastating war. She believed that science should be used to make life better, not worse for people. She refused to use her knowledge and talent to aid a war. To this day, when scientists examine the moral issues around their discoveries, Clara Immerwahr's ideas are discussed.

In a lot of ways, she was ahead of her time. It was a hard life for her, being so different from other women. Always use your gifts to help other people and you can be like empathetic Clara Immerwahr!

Clara Breed was an ordinary librarian who became a hero to children and teenagers at a time when they needed her most. She was born in Iowa in 1906, and after she graduated from college, she became a librarian in San Diego.

Clara Breed was loved by the many children and teenagers who visited her library. Then in 1941, life changed for Americans when Japan attacked Pearl Harbor, drawing the United States into World War II. In the hysteria that followed the attack, United States officials decided to relocate Japanese Americans all over the West Coast to internment camps, which was like prison. The decision was racist and made from fear.

Among the 120,000 Japanese Americans who were forced to leave their homes and move into the camps were Clara Breed's young friends who came to her library. Wanting to help them, she gave them stamped and addressed post cards on the day they boarded a train leaving San Diego. She told them to write as soon as they could so that they could be pen pals.

The letters from the children and teenagers began pouring in, telling her about their hard experiences in the camps, their fears, and frustrations. She wrote back to all of them, sending care packages that included soap, toothbrushes and library books. She traveled to visit them at the internment camps too. Her visits, kind words, packages and books lifted the children's spirits while they were there. She received over 250 letters from her young pen pals in the internment camps. The letters written between Clara Breed and the children are now on display at The Japanese American National Museum in California!

Clara Breed also wrote letters to government officials on her friends' behalf. She told them that people should not be sent to internment camps because of their ancestry. She wrote articles that were published in magazines on the topic too. The Japanese American people were released from internment camps in 1946, after World War II ended. Years later, the United States government addressed their wrongdoing and apologized for mistreating Japanese Americans.

Clara Breed was a hero because she was an advocate for her friends. One day, your friends may need you to advocate for them too. If that day comes, be a friend like Clara Breed!

This page is all about you!

_____ was born on

_____

As a baby, Clara _____

_____

As a little girl, Clara _____

_____

Clara is especially good at _____

_____

Clara is often described as _____

_____

Clara makes people laugh when she _____

_____

One day Clara would like to _____

_____

This page is for making a self-portrait. A self-portrait is a picture of you, drawn by you!

Bibliography

Dick, Jutta. "Clara Immerwahr." *Jewish Women: A Comprehensive Historical Encyclopedia*. Jewish Women's Archive. 1 Mar. 2009. Web. 24 Jun 2018

The Editors of biography.com, "Clara Brown Biography." *The biography.com website*. A&E Television Networks. 21 Sep. 2015. Web. 24 Jun 2018

The Editors of Encyclopaedia Britannica, "Clara Barton." *Encyclopaedia Britannica*. Encyclopaedia Britannica, inc. 16 Apr. 2018. Web. 24 Jun. 2018

The Editors of Encyclopaedia Britannica, "Clara Bow." *Encyclopaedia Britannica*. Encyclopaedia Britannica, inc. 09 Mar. 2018. Web. 24 Jun. 2018

The Editors of Encyclopaedia Britannica, "Clara Hughes." *Encyclopaedia Britannica*. Encyclopaedia Britannica, inc. 31 Aug. 2017. Web. 24 Jun. 2018

The Editors of Encyclopaedia Britannica, "Clara Schumann." *Encyclopaedia Britannica*. Encyclopaedia Britannica, inc. 17 May. 2018. Web. 24 Jun. 2018

Librarian Clara Breed. Uncommon Ground: Japanese American Internment. *Library.miracosta.edu.* Miracosta College Library. 31 August 2022. Web. 26 Sep 2023.

Wikipedia contributors. "Clara (given name)." *Wikipedia, The Free Encyclopedia*. Wikipedia, The Free Encyclopedia, 9 May. 2018. Web. 24 Jun. 2018.

Wikipedia contributors. "Clara Breed." *Wikipedia, The Free Encyclopedia*. Wikipedia, The Free Encyclopedia, 15 Feb. 2023. Web. 27 Sep. 2023.

Wikipedia contributors. "Clare of Assisi." *Wikipedia, The Free Encyclopedia.* Wikipedia, The Free Encyclopedia, 24 May. 2018. Web. 24 Jun. 2018

Wikipedia contributors. "Clara Barton." *Wikipedia, The Free Encyclopedia.* Wikipedia, The Free Encyclopedia, 15 Jun. 2018. Web. 24 Jun. 2018

Wikipedia contributors. "Clara Bow." *Wikipedia, The Free Encyclopedia.* Wikipedia, The Free Encyclopedia, 12 Jun. 2018. Web. 24 Jun. 2018

Wikipedia contributors. "Clara Brown." *Wikipedia, The Free Encyclopedia.* Wikipedia, The Free Encyclopedia, 8 May. 2018. Web. 24 Jun. 2018

Wikipedia contributors. "Clara Hughes." *Wikipedia, The Free Encyclopedia.* Wikipedia, The Free Encyclopedia, 9 May. 2018. Web. 24 Jun. 2018

Wikipedia contributors. "Clara Immerwahr." *Wikipedia, The Free Encyclopedia.* Wikipedia, The Free Encyclopedia, 8 Jun. 2018. Web. 24 Jun. 2018.

Wikipedia contributors. "Clara Schumann." *Wikipedia, The Free Encyclopedia.* Wikipedia, The Free Encyclopedia, 21 Jun. 2018. Web. 24 Jun. 2018

www.ingramcontent.com/pod-product-compliance
Lightning Source LLC
Chambersburg PA
CBHW042110040426
42448CB00002B/217